A Passable Man

A PASSABLE MAN
Poems

Ralph Culver

MADHAT PRESS
CHESHIRE, MASSACHUSETTS

For Tiara,
Thanks for the
kicking intro!
All the best,

Ralph
Culver

MadHat Press
MadHat Incorporated
PO Box 422, Cheshire, MA 01225

The Library of Congress has assigned
this edition a Control Number of
2021947317

ISBN 978-1-952335-29-7 (paperback)

Text by Ralph Culver
Author photo by Hilary Appelman
Cover design by Ralph Culver
Cover image: *Seiltänzer* [Tightrope Walker], 1923, by Paul Klee.
Copyright the Estate of Paul Klee. Used by permission.

www.madhat-press.com

First Printing

Printed in the United States of America

Also by Ralph Culver

Both Distances

So Be It

For my children and grandchildren

To the memory of my parents

Table of Contents

IV

V

There is only this dark
and the familiar place of my body.
And the voices calling out
of me for love.
                    —JACK GILBERT

And how shall we survive? We don't and cannot and will never
Know.
                    —HAYDEN CARRUTH

Prelude

Come winter. Autumn pockets
her colors, pulls up
the once warm roots
and hunches southward: a gray,
drained hand rises. Shadow. Shadow.
It stops the blood. It stops
the brain's fragile traffic. It stops

a buck, rumping a doe
grazing near fast water. He lifts
a tentative hoof and peers.
Every November that he began
waiting to starve is coming in
on the cold purpose of this wind.

And I count the times
I could not keep from turning
to check, mid-step,
the footprints strung behind
in the climbing snow.

I

Taking Bluegill at Lake Seneca

for my sister and cousins

Under the weight of a few rocks
and the unmerciful heat of midday
they lie: eight bejeweled beauties
aligned on the edge of the dock,
the first five utterly still,
the two next murmuring at the gills,
and the last not quite reduced
to commentary but yet in the vale
of acts and action. A tremor
shudders his length to the tail,
the caudal fin taut and quaking,
and I suddenly feel a memory
fall through me of what it meant
to consider surrender, remembering
swimming for shore on a dare,
our rowboat out too far
and the sound of thunder nearing;
a limitless pain and fear
deep in my thighs and calves
so pathologically engraved there
I stare down at my bare legs
in wonder, and laugh.
But I am young,
and so these fish are young,
this water with its battered skin is young,
the trees surrounding, young—

even my father and mother are young.
Soon the eighth captive is left
no belief in escape,
but speaks instead his conviction
of infinite release.
I will not be the one
to flay them naked
or scuttle the flawless heads
in the minnow bucket for the coons.
I will not touch them again
except to eat them.
                    So speech is mine.
The first words are small
and have a taste of hook,
the sting of a pearl of wine.

Fill Up

Lulled, he sits, a nothing in the vast
back seat, amid the drumming of the gasoline,
the stunned smell of worn felt and Marlboros.
Two heedless growths perch on their collared stems,
murmur the day and will not turn. Between
them, the air bends out above the hood, the way
a snake sends itself across the surface of a lake.
He studies his debased reflection in
the chrome plate of an ashtray, mounted damaged
at the center of his parents' seat before him.
Gulf. He slowly leans into that face:
it swells, narrows, and runs down
the cracked silver. One voice enlarges,
saying "Watch it, honey, or you're going
to be replaced." A laugh. A cough.
They are always almost there. Where are they taking
him? How could I, waiting for whatever
was to happen to happen, how
could I not see where they were taking him?

Round

The fire is not particular.
The storm knows no names.
The wave cannot tell the child and stone apart.
The fire craves only hunger.

The storm is not one to keep secrets.
The wave knows the child and stone share a skin.
The fire cannot feed without eating its home.
The storm craves a sky larger than this.

The wave is not the child's notion of shelter, the stone's notion
      of breath.
The fire knows no single answer will do.
The storm cannot speak without dying a little.
The wave craves the loss of itself.

Beneath the window the fire trembles.
Beneath the window the storm hurls its black toys.
Beneath the window the wave lowers itself to its knees.
Beneath the window the child bends over the stone,
sings *My mommy my daddy my mommy.*

Boy at the Plate

for my children, and for my parents

Spread, the boy's legs are unsteady
as tent poles in a squall.
It is useless to tell him
I know what this is,
waiting on someone who seems
as near as the end of his reach
to give him his chance
at shame. That he hardly believes
it is himself: I heard that voice
in my head so many times
it became a weapon,
the only weapon I had.
It is useless to tell him
the same voice splits from the throat
of the field mouse, rearing up
to teeth as long as its own forelegs—
useless, and wrong. For now,
the boy must believe he stands
in the mouth of the first fear
birthed in the world. Later,
in time, perhaps while
watching his own and shaken by
the glory of it that it is,
he will see for himself
the common fear, the common love
he fell out of, now into,
and watch, and love, and be thankful.

Totem

*One fall day, J., a boy of eleven, found the decomposing body of a
dog. It appeared to have been dead for some time. The boy worked
the dog's head off the carcass, shoved a tree branch in at the neck,
and carried the head down through some woods into an adjacent
public playground.*

This new spine screwed tight
in the under-pulp
of a skull, formerly
dog—as an invention of meaning
in your hands,

it makes sense. The park trees
beginning to smolder with autumn colors
jangle and jag:
the possible beauty of things
pisses you off. Your mouth waters
at the lift and bell
of young girls on the seesaw,
but there's this terror
of whatever's pushing the black hair
outward at your armpits and balls,
and who understands it at all?

Left no choice,
you came down out of
the oak and locust trees,
head high, leering,
spittlish and lousy,
concessively marking your borders—

your little corner of hell
in September, school just on
and just out that day,
down to the playground
and the children who must
recall it better than I.

Ralph Culver

The Tinies

for *Thomas Lux*

Bless them, bless them,
the tinies:
sipping a drop of tea from an acorn cap,
changing a flat on a Lego car
the color of daffodils—

how I love them, the tinies,
always on the lookout for
the blind foot, the mouse
sozzled and reeling from the meat
of a turned apple.

This one digs down
through her handbag:
one pea-skin.
"Do you have the keys, Harry?"

The tinies, the tinies,
who will care for them?
Who will help paint their living rooms
with a blueberry?
Who can possibly tie their shoes
if they hurt their fingers?

The tinies skip stones in the birdbath,
set sail across a swimming pool
with a week's worth of provisions,
meticulously catalogued....

Oh, you tinies,
who will protect you?
Danger is a storm the size of a hat,
death waits in the black thread
of shadow that trails
from a needle of grass—

and yet, and yet,
they know
it is a world of joy,
these tinies,
large as it is,
large as it is.

Tableau

A boy lies on his stomach on the floor, head propped up on his left hand, drawing in a sketchbook with his right—so far, only a line or two, just a suggestion of a shape.

Over near the window, sitting at his desk, a man stares at a sheet of paper rolled into a typewriter. A few words are there, nothing substantial.

And the third figure in the room, whose very form is nascent, untroubled by detail—nearly transparent, really? Although the man and the boy sense a presence, acknowledge it, they pay it no mind, confident as they are, as you are reading this, as I am writing it, that now is not the time the figure congeals, casting a shadow at last, and rises to take his measure.

The First

I seal
the light out
with a breath.
A wax-run clots
to a pearl
on the dresser.

The crickets' song goes
around and around
your face, drawing
me down. We gather
in the space of our flesh
to witness
what never can happen again,
not ever:

the flushed sweat caught;
your cupped belly;
my thin bones
colliding with

death. Mine. *Mine.*

But now
I thank the dead
for those first clues.

II

Bargainers

for Louise Glück

In the market, Saturday, the world's commerce on the simplest
      terms,
terms anyone can understand. Hanks of dried chilies
like garlands of tongues, baskets of Roma tomatoes in the
      noon sun,
warm and firm to the touch.

A young man leans against the stone facade of the pastry shop
under the shade of a window awning.
He is trying to catch the eye of the girl selling the tomatoes
while an old couple haggles with her about the price
and when the tomatoes were picked.
The young man lights a thin cigar; it's black, slightly bent,
as though he were setting fire to an oak twig in his mouth.

He shakes out the match and snaps it into the street in one
      movement,
a gesture he had seen in a film as a child and never forgotten:
some actor in a narrow tie and lapels and steel-rimmed
      sunglasses.
A doomed hero, not too bright really, although this hadn't
      mattered
in the least—sheer determination and purpose, that was what
      counted.
The details of the story, the movie's title—a movie as old

as the young man's parents, maybe older—
all that's forgotten.

As every Saturday, the girl sees the boy clearly—a blossom of
       flame,
the matchstick spinning out of the shadows and into the
       sunlight—
even now, as she tries to reassure the couple the tomatoes are
       fresh.
On the vine this morning, on the vine this morning,
she repeats. Two thick ropes of smoke begin idly paying out
       the boy's nostrils,
braiding upward in the midday stillness. And then in one
       movement
she snaps a paper bag open and begins to fill it with tomatoes
as the old couple points: this one, this one. This one.

Warsaw Rocks, New York Takes Note

When the man in the mine-light
hammers on the Stratocaster,
you're in the middle of fucking
and stop.
       "What?" *Plumbing.*
                Then,
dumb. Ah, acquiescence: too much
Henry Miller. In bed, in her, the 19th floor;
you wonder, what is that in feet?
That's how it is in great cities.
The jewelry of copper tubing, elbow-joints,
and faucetry posit that meat and shit
are beauty—just it. Singing, he has
too many c's and z's, but singing all the same.
Everything's familiar: the world *is* culture.
Red bones, white flag. The stroke of genius.
In feet: about two hundred. She comes exactly.

Dancing Down Broadway with My Bottle of Brandy

for Danny Seidenberg

I

Sober, you continued
to be repulsive. Another,
she in green, senses the need
you sense and pivots, pursuing
an immediate elsewhere. Turns
one eye to the topmost
of two pulses wed
at her wrist; confirms
she's history, from
either approach. What
it is, it's—you think—
too obvious. Things tend
to support this conclusion
in spite of your demand for little,
if not nothing,
from any. Then
her buttressed foot discerned
at the logical end of a last glance
falls, without thought,
just beyond the potential glee
of a fresh dog-pile
that squats dead center in
a streetlight's wisdom.
You think of vaudeville

and several Eastern religions.
You think life is
basically stupid. You
go home with this weight,
fat with retreat, and
break out the last bottle.

II

You skiffle on the rain-spat paving, swing
the amber-dancing club about your head,
a warning and a benediction. Dread
confines: you've finished with it. Now you wing
your way through these convenient double doors,
approach the bench. Two close-clung counselors
take brief stock of their virtues; compromise
is obviously ordered. *His* and *Hers*
their dewy steins announce. MacNelly's eyes
appraise your burden. His fat finger points
at your specific self. He smiles. "The joint's
just closed," he says, "as far as you're concerned."
The chatter dims. If nothing else, you've learned
when you're not wanted. Your teeth by the girl's
feet you envisage, a matched set of pearls
broken and scattered in some jug-room fray.
Your company in hand, you turn away.

That's that. Back
in the street the rain

Ralph Culver

dies quietly. An old pain
sparks. Two men
waiting for a bus, a drunk
snores in his swollen clothes: the obvious
again speaking, that rough,
unquiet diamond. And

of the other, of love,
there is never, never enough.

Black Sneakers

The window over her shoulder.
I thought: *This light.*

God, she said.

The light was just about perfect.
I admired its precision,
its hold on things.
My black sneakers—
soon I would be in them.
Where next? I wondered.
What did they have in mind?

God, she said,
I can feel you
up in my stomach.

To you, of course.
They will take me
to you, and the world
in my shadow will become
yet more beautiful,
as it does
to all prisoners.
More dangerous.

Ralph Culver

You Do What You're Good At

Half beached, half borne
on the pond's jade palm, to the neck
in lakes and thundered over
by water shorn from high rock,
on pool tables, in the backs
of vehicles stilled and moving,
upright or hunched over
in every room, kitchen, living, bath,
laundry, foyer, den and dining,
and in beds on floors, beds
that hung suspended from cables,
beds of straw, spring and water,
cotton, flannel and satin,
in crash-pads and under canopies
with breakfast and roses,
by log and candle, sun and moon,
and in the sweep of a thousand lamps
bearing off darkness of varying degree
they are moaning over me, under me,
before and behind me, the list
of those having had none better
growing longer as I sing
Back, Death, back,
only knowing you do what you're good at,
knowing dying
is what I am doing here.

Caterer

peeling free my skin
how happy I am
panels of muscle   fat
slapped down on the block

stripping out channels   canals
skeins of vein and vessel
the joy
as my eyes trundle away

she laughs with me
while I decouple vertebrae
now my tongue humps off
soundlessly trailing saliva

soon all that remain
brain   heart
this dilating keystone
bowlful of tremulant jelly

clenching the brain
where her legs fork
my heart she eats
bright cables of blood unspool

in the glow of white tapers
breath of cut peonies
how happy I am
at her pleasure

27

her mouth gorged with
the last gesture
the final thought
painting her thighs

Resolute

after Jack Gilbert

The towering sun. Screaming whiteness high above the sea.
The light-stropped waves along Long Island Sound, curved
        blades
ranked and relentlessly advancing. That whiteness. The gesso
Alex layered across another canvas, one she had stretched
some nights before. How her eyes ground shut and teeth
        gritted
when I moved inside her, as if she were dragging a great weight.
Three of us, living in rooms barely adequate for one.
Not that the baby and I will be there much longer. Thinking
of my vast hunger set loose by the smell of boiled eggs
that slid across the Parkway East as I rode beside my father
driving into Pittsburgh. Flame-tipped stacks of the J&L mills
decanting smoke, sulfur pouring into the Ford through
the open windows. Just fourteen, famished, wondering what
would become of us, certain I heard the clink of empties
jostling in a case of beer in the trunk behind the back seat.
Praying the university might let him keep his job. Or not.
If we open ourselves to quintessence rather than particulars
we gain in clarity, the way a bee does not recall a flower
but does its purposeful gavotte to point the way
to an abundance. Spinning under the blows of the sun,
helpless, the dazzling white sand ablaze beneath my feet.
This helplessness that will set me to flight again
already beginning to resolve in me as anticipation.
Pleasurable expectancy. A kind of contentment.

How It Happens Sometimes

On finding a note
he has left her,
the woman lugs
their mattress down
three flights of stairs
and touches fire to it
in the driveway.
This is how night comes,
an animal that wants
your blood, that wants
to wear your skin
like a summer dress.
We run. But there's no place to go.
Flame and rancor
render love to a slag nest
strewn with coiled bone.
Scraps of ash twist
in cold ascent
like stricken butterflies.

Tabernacle

a smear of red
sunset her menstrual blood
sings on my tongue

irises
unfold coursing spring
blossoms in her eyes

my whole life
this is my temple
deep breath and tears

what is the name for it
the name we give it
one breath one tear after another

leading to this welcome
stillness
welcome dust

she sleeps
I rise I go
to wash at the river

dust becoming
breath becoming
water

the sky stretched over us
vestment beneath which
all dust all water

passeth

The Dress

A narrow dirt road in a coastal town
finds a man lying down beneath a scrub tree
by the shoulder, near enough to the sea
to hear its plunge and plow. The ground
is hard; the man arches his back a bit
and settles. Across his face and chest
rests the shadow of the tree; it
trembles barely, and the man—doing his best
to create a more forgiving place—tries
to imagine the shade and the scrub tree
as something else. But the shade slipping over him lightly
becomes a black dress the tree might just
have stepped free of, and the breath of the sea
at his ear is a lover's sleep, and then
there is no helping it.
The earth is too hard. Though he can't move quite yet,
the man is walking, walking in himself, already down
this road that leaves him now,
under the folds of the dress.

III

Reassurance

May everything be true:
the rubric of fire, face
and body settling,
your arm around my neck
urging me to you.
Modus vivendi. Grace,
despite our meddling,
holds doubt in check.
May everything be true,
and truth direct.

In Early Spring

for Hil

The river has overrun its banks, as happens
most Aprils. Undoing the laces of her shoe,
he slides his palm slowly from her ankle
up her calf to behind her knee, her skin
warm against his hand. He thinks of a family
of white-tailed deer crossing the wetlands near
the mouth of the river. Now his hand along
her inner thigh. Their heads lowered, they stand
in a few inches of icy water
and nibble at the young green shoots. Only
occasionally do they raise their gaze
toward the trees to scan for threatening
forms. Then, detecting none, she touches him.
Everything they need is there before them.

The Misunderstanding

I did not say: *You are nothing to me;*
I said the hummingbird, the anglerfish
are not amazed at themselves.

I did not say: *I have forgotten you;*
but that every day a man
finds more things that trouble him.

Not *You are not beautiful,*
but that, often, when I lie in the grass,
a lute sings in the earth beneath me.

Not: *I regret*—
but that I stare at these keys
I carry in my pocket
and think of the narrow bones
I once turned over in the garden.

Not *I never loved you,*
but *You are all you have.*

As for the rest, yes,
it is as you say, the words
are mine, but all the rooms of the world
we have lived in close now
over the words of others.
Earth, keys, man—

when will you seek out
that lamp, that light,
under which they were written?

Her Heart, Morning

for Hil

The roses have used up their time on Earth.
Well, for now. In five months
spring will have its say. But today the snow
has changed everything—hiding despair
and promise equally. The light, increasing
from the east, frames her at the window
as she looks down on the featureless yard
beneath its white, obscurant mantle.
What to feel? she wonders, that space
in her chest noncommittal,
even though she senses how much the man
in the bed behind her loves her.
What to feel, when what we have
is good and still not what we wanted?
She understands: she desires a sign—
a cardinal alighting on the branch just
beneath the sill. Maybe the dog will bark or
a rabbit will cross the yard by the trunk
of the maple. In the meantime,
waiting, she sees just clearly enough
that she needn't choose despair
or promise, one over the other, just now.
His breathing is even. A constancy.
Her own breath fogs the windowpane.

Koan of a Sort

The sounds of water as she rises from her bath
while I slice bread in the kitchen:
How can I still feel sorry for myself?

The Gardenia

for Sandra Merkel

You tend. Water
slips from the sheened
leaves. The quick wedge,
silvered in houselight,
wells down, a blade
urging it thrive; hands rise
with the lessening.
The weight passes from
living to living. There is
no end to this. And
that flowering winter,
the flesh and scent
I can't sort from my own.
Familiar. No longer real.

Paramouria

You know (you think), and then
you think you know you don't,
and then all you know is only
that you think you need to know.
You think: the kids know. Friends.
Your father hints at it.
Elected officials huddle, murmuring.
And so: you, tightening down the cap
of spermicide, exacting
alignment of the marks
on top and tube you have etched
with a diaper pin;
you, propping with grim purpose
the diaphragm case against
the cluttered, innocent
inhabitants of the medicine cabinet,
awaiting some skewing disturbance
of urgency and precaution—
a precise haphazardry
against which any chance
of happenstantial re-creation
all odds are.
Some days you
scrutinize this craftsmanship
more than once. You
begin to notice you spend
more time than ever
out of the house. She acts

as though this concerns her
but you are being guileful,
providing opportunity. And so:
a wretch, self-sickened,
you sit alone in bars,
oblivious to the sidelong come-on,
the whispered *Hey there*, and
sweat away the hours, head home
to a greeting of unmatched
passion and intensity. You fuck
as though you were inventing
the wheel. And after? While you
piss more on the bathroom floor
than not as you stretch
to reset the snare behind
the mirrored door, she
lies pooling the crushed sheets,
beside herself, afire, certain
in her apprehension:
the foreign perfume that she swore she traced
along *your* collar bones describes
a flaming arc, an accusative cascade
of sparks, across
the American night!

Digit

Stumbling on the stairs, he sees how the slashed crosshatching
      of late-autumn branches
explodes in a boiling mass of spooked birds at the same
      moment his hand
trying to catch the sill of the window goes through the glass,
and he cannot help himself but to think of how a school of
      smaller fish,
pilchard perhaps, sardines, or whatever those silvery daggers
      are that spume and spiral
with common consciousness in the depths of the oceans like a
      time-lapse cloud
suddenly changing course again and again, escape easily
      through the purse seine
scaled for a larger catch, the nets tightening below the surface
      and drawing closed
as the window splinters to a graph tracking his fortunes in
      this volatile lifetime,
good year, bad year, good year, very bad year, his father leaves
      his mother,
he meets his wife, his child is born, the drinking starts again,
      until he leaves his wife
now descending naked in a postcoital, orgastic, self-satisfied
      shambles and earns this momentary glimpse
of the lurking dread that always culminates in balance wrack
      and panic: captured, freed,
the end of his right index finger lopped instantly, bloodlessly
      resting in the double-

paned debris unmanicured and still fresh with the bleach-
      smell of semen,
pointing up and out at the numerous black forms that already
      have resettled in the trees.

Confessional

Now is no time to forget
what I know: no one,
once loved, ever leaves you.
She comes into the house
from an unyielding blackness
that has no gifts, only secrets.
A book lies open on my knees.
The door shuts, makes a sound
pleading for silence.
Now she sits. Neither moves,
yet the floor moans
as though someone walked there
around something they dare not awaken.
Now she stares at a print on the wall
that for years she has forgotten
even existed.
Now there is going to be trouble.

The Song of the Open Marriage

The dinner's done; the table clear.
The father takes a moment's pause.
The baby sheds a tired tear
as in the bedroom Mother draws
a trail of scent behind each ear.

The eldest child buffs dishes dry;
the middle child imparts a frown
(the book report she can't put by);
as dusk casts stars above the town
the father casts a darkening eye.

But Baby's cheered, for Dad's about
to read a book—whate'er she chooses.
Mister Edward Bear, the stout?
Or Horton, and his silly Whoses?
Mother says, "I'm going out."

The children pay her little mind—
it happens one night every week.
They think her not the least unkind,
but take their kisses on the cheek
and turn to what she leaves behind.

The dishes clean, the pen put down,
the baby gets a final prance
as Father hunts her flannel gown,
while Mother eases off her pants
on the other side of town.

49

"Come children, come. It's nine o'clock,"
as Father turns the bedding out.
The children brush their teeth and talk
while, elsewhere, sheets crack in the rout
as Mother makes the mattress rock.

A blackness climbs across the pane—
the petals of the night seal up
around the house. A widening stain
of moonlight fills the shaking cup
that Father empties. They have lain

not long enough, but must adieux.
The pact's specific: her return
is what she has agreed with you.
The rest we leave for flame to burn
or for the ever-turning screw

to mate the truths we never learn.
Tomorrow Daddy has his due.

Nocturne

The woman on the bed
should have been weeping, but no,
it's the man by the window,
one hand on the sill, head down,

as on either side of him
lace curtains furl upon
the sudden absence of wind
that had stirred the cloth wildly

and then ceased, a caprice
of the summer air lost
on both of them. His face
shines, shines with tears,

mercurous tributaries
feeding a larger malice
than he knows, although
in the reach of lamplight

he begins to see. How vast
and deepening, this abyss
of expedient contempt,
as he turns on her at last.

The Last

I
For the peace
of one night's easy passage,
I burned all
that my name had brought me;
all that I had
I put into memory
to make light enough
I might see you by—

for the near-sleep coming of you,
not a word; not the sound
of *the rose* but
the rose. The steady pulse
lifted across years
and led back to silence.

II
See   the moon is out
rocking the river
to sleep

The moon is out
horned
silver basket   I
will a flower into
its bright cup
See how my dying is taken
by you

III

I crush my one promise.

I swear to defend the ruins.

Field in Winter

I had thought
what a poor thing it was
to have loved and lost

Yet in some part of me
I am wishing him well
the man in your bed tonight

the care of your happiness
now entrusted to him

And the tracks in the snow
They mark
both distances

from and to

The new snow will come
What happens then
any child knows

No evidence of our passing

Lyric

The bird makes its nest.
It has reasons. It is alive.
You want to leave it alone.

The bird,
a few threads in its beak.

I love this peace. It
is like burning.

IV

The Woman in the Plant Shop

for Ginni Stern

I

She is moving among them, singing
easefully, randomly dissonant,
singing, song touching each,
and touching each
the song-attending leaves; the earth-worn
hands, gentle, quick,
ride the beam-framed harbor
of unrelenting green. Rootsure,
tuned to the vying needs,
her whole music falls, a blessing
indiscriminate as rain. Given
to giving, she routs death
from the growth, singing; sings

though in her own wanting, she,
and bred with death as any.

II

Bolt fast, the keys chime
on the steel ring: day done.
Above her, as ever,
heaven is conjuring its stars.
Before her, their brothers,
her charges—small flames

back of the blackened glass
rising in blind accomplishment
through season on season.

Pep Talk

Heather McHugh, for and after

Opinion
is your wing,
what binds you,
the small cog in a very big machine,
the pinecone's plaits
of armour.
Appeal? Sister,
that original skin
fits you like a frock
you're just breaking in.
Habitude is everything,
diamond-heart—
we're made to suit
ourselves. We
want to feel,
inside, at home. Me, I
feel the thought
of you and (having come
hither) make you
here a mend of words,
utter delight. You have to
trust, you have to
trust what goes.
Trust me: what goes
is what becomes us.

Seamstress

Belief in the thread consoles, redeems. The warm
ease of your ceaseless hands draws down
the twill-flecked light. Beyond the windowpane,
stars shred themselves and drift across silk, seams for
your later eyes to follow. Now,

deft in work, the blue irises feed through
each pass of the needle, riddle the
carcass of the cotton-flower. There is
always work, and always another hour. Your
spare form, clothed in a loose blouse and
the sweating air: stale and harried, yet
rising, constellated with the remnant sparks. You,
only sewing. Something else is joined together.

Glassblower

for Leslie Baker

Like that other god who breathed life into fire and molten dust, she rests.

It is good to stand here, thinking of nothing, to be still under the caress of the world's essential sensuousness.

Her face, neck, and back damp with sweat. Sipping water from a white china mug.

Her face and neck damp from squarely confronting the furnace.

Turned now toward the heavy steel grid of the old factory windows vented at an angle, she stares out at the falling snow. The firelight behind her touching off sparks of lavender and indigo across the coursing snowflakes.

Lavender and indigo glistening at the nape of her neck, she drinks. Breathing deeply and slowly in the ravishment of the chill, glittering snow before her and the heat of the furnace pressing at her back.

She sets her empty cup down on a cluttered table, and returns to the making.

A Go at the Lifting-stone

*For many years a nearly round granite stone about two feet in
diameter sat at the easterly corner of the front steps of the store
now owned by Frank E. Brown. Few men in the town could lift it
off the ground.*
—Fred Pitkin, History of Marshfield, Vermont, 1947

The hands, arms, shoulders and back
consult briefly. A new challenge
of some dimension, of serious intent.
Promise heaves in the brain. This
is our provincial glory!
The bet down—budge it, and you won't
have to buy your own beer for a week—
you think, in a sense, your future
lies bearing its secret under the stone,
the days breaking in your favor
or not an equation of space—
its possibilities—
conjuncting with the flesh
and its limitations;
all borne up forever on the skin
of the earth, a place that seems
suddenly new and somehow
getting younger by the minute
until you have the confirmation
you seek. By God,

you are about to *learn* something
(this being your sole duty);

and you learn something sure enough.
Next day, when the usual warriors
clap you on the armored brace,
your lips roll back like a dog's—
the bloody thing having not given
an inch. The sudden multitude
of flea-like urgencies in your ankle
you would rather die than bend
to attend to. Closing your eyes to this
and the uncompromising grins
stretched across the faces of
these yahoos buying you
beer after beer after beer.

Zoar

> *And Lot said … Behold now, this city is near to flee unto, and it*
> *is a little one: Oh, let me escape thither, (is it not a little one?) and*
> *my soul shall live.*
>   —Genesis 19:18-20

A little town, and you know how it is—
everyone knows everyone and everybody's business—
so when the stranger and his two preening tarts arrived
we gave them a good look. One old, old man
in rags, eyes always on the verge of panic,
a face the sun had churned to bearded pitch.
Muttering, rapt, he wouldn't meet your gaze,
and I thought, *This one is going to be a problem.* Still,
it was the girls—no better dressed, but young,
straight-backed, smug and teasing—who gave me
the most pause. Sisters to each other, we assumed,
but their companion, that cowed derelict, could hardly
be the father of those two, with no one playing
wife or mother in their company. And so
we guessed they were two whores arrived from Sodom,
enslaved to this decrepit pimp the heat and years
had bent into a fool. Later, my brother's
hips gripped tightly in my sweating hands,
it came to me to cut the old man's throat
and keep the girls myself. But blessed lust
and drink made sleep of my ambitions;
all praise! For by dusk the shouting had brought us
to the roofs to watch the soundless flame and smoke
devouring the obliterated distance.

No one saw them leave, the girls and the old man,
but they were gone; no doubt fear or some surmise
set them to flight. Had I followed them
to carry out my plans I might have died.
It was four days before the scouts returned with word
that nothing stood of the cities of the plain,
only ashes, the charred bones of livestock.
Not a shrub or tree, across fused and blackened sands
as finely polished as a shield; no tracks
leading to our gates but what the scouts themselves
had made. Zoar alone remains—the only sign
of human life beyond our walls a crumbled stump
of salt that some lost trader left behind,
that beasts have gnawed away to nearly nothing.

For the Last Catamount

The round, descending
eye of fire narrows down
the gun-sight valley.
A hawk hangs perfectly still,
then sheers toward the river.

Day-heavy, lazing
on a warming rock, the gold
head of teeth and thick-
lidded opals shifts, yawning
under the sun's attentions.

Her paws go soft now.
She dozes. Skirling blackflies
and the quick water's
reassuring purl meld to
a rustle of parting growth.

She recognizes
what can only be summoned
in dreams: his likeness
driven from and nearing her.
He stands in wait by the trees.

Night and hunger, one
being, will fall soon enough,
patiently hunting
the mouth of the river to
follow the valley upstream.

She wakens without
expectation. Water, kill,
sleep, the passing light—
the labors of a daily
birth, in a world of endings.

Sundown Coming, and the Hummingbird Is Called Home

I
How suddenly the air has cooled

Rain gives thanks
and joins its forebears
plunging drop by silver drop
into the trout pond

As the sky clears
stars begin to follow
in the paths of the rain

II
Somewhere
molded from leaf bits
and bound around with caterpillar web
and the beard-silk of tall grasses
a cup
the size of a vole's bedroll
trembles in the fork
of a slender bough
cradles two eggs

They glint
like lost beads
of a child's bracelet

Embers from the fire spark downward
stutter and whisper
to the attentive earth
by where these boots stand
drying

Pause at Dusk: Dragging the New Eden River for the Body of a Missing Canoeist

Downriver an eddy took the skiff
where it notched in the stone off the eastern bank.
I watch from upstream as a red cross rises
from it, then another, stretched taut
and stark on the green of the boatmen's coats,
and recall two targets on a gray ridge,
long ago. I had just unstrung my bow
under the sun's last bolts
and bull's-eyes' glare, and marked
how every flare of color in the dun world draws:
the bee to the mountain flower, the rifle barrel
to the gaudy square of cloth
pinned to the chest of the prisoner.
Through that remembered brilliance,
blazed, they offer themselves,
but a tension to the current pulls me back.
I lean to the line and see—
as though I were the one who had seen it—
the paddle a man has spotted from shore
near Bristol, four miles below:
white, a carmine band about the blade,
alone in a circle of water.

V

Camping Alone

As you lean toward the fire, the flames reach out to you, and you think of your mother at the kitchen sink holding a rinsed dinner plate up to the light of late afternoon. How she sensed you watching her there from the hall doorway, wearing your mantle of dirt and sweat that you wrapped yourself in every summer day at the ball field. But now the fire is guttering down, and you begin to feel the thin layer of grief that settles on everything, almost a fragrance, reminding you that memory, always memory and nothing else, is the only fuel available to you to stoke the embers back into a blaze.

Ralph Culver

Three Poems for My Father
Monty Culver, 1929–2009

Lashed

Binding himself to the mast as the storm
comes on, tying the paintbrushes to hands
knotted with arthritis and time. I don't
somehow think so. He was more like,
Fuck that. I'm done with these goddamned words.
And still he had his way with them
to the end. Over the phone I always asked
if he was reading any new writer
he could recommend. The last
time, before it became clear he
thought I was his nephew Steve,
he said, *Jane Austen.* That sly, that artful,
that funny. Having his way with them,
like a father coaxing his child to eat.
Like a father coaxing his child to smile.

Skill without Action: Silk Kite, No Wind

He answered in a letter, after I'd wondered
if he was doing any writing, that he was
working on some poetry, but no one
has yet turned up a line of it. Because,
of course, he wasn't writing anything.
One dry, lying drunk knowing the other
dry, lying drunk is lying. Loving
language, but thirsting for nuance. Only
the sentence gives you that, he knew. Only
the holy sentence. But only on the page.

Fishing with My Father, and the Craft of Poetry

Hours holding the poles over the water,
hours of catching nothing or not much,
and throwing back what we did catch.
What the hell was that about, anyway?
And yet today I have this patience
for things that drive some people crazy:
standing in line at the supermarket,
waiting for some fool blowhard to stop gabbing,
searching for a coat button in the snow.
The finely honed conviction that beneath
this nothing is a deeper, richer nothing.
Consecrating myself to the silence, and then
to what interrupts the silence.

Certitude

Mary Culver, 1922–1996

My mother in her pale-blue bathing suit, a one-piece the same tone as the summer Pennsylvania sky above, her back to the camera, seated on a blanket in the grass by the pond's edge. The day is bright, and the wide-brimmed hat shades her as well as concealing her face from the lens. There are three ducks on the water to her right, grouped close together, and though her face is hidden it's quite obvious from the angle of her shoulders and the cant of the hat brim that her full attention is on them. I have examined this photograph closely on numerous occasions, and each time I do I remember an evening when we were browsing through the album together at the dining-room table, and when we came to this picture she softly touched the edge of the print with her hand. As though asking herself if she had ever been happier than she was in that moment, and knowing the answer, and saying nothing, and I watch her face as she turns the page of the album gently, but with purpose. The matter settled.

Last Call

What the mind fashions, what the mind does not,
she says, but no way I'm being sucked into that dialectic.
A freezing wind follows someone through the door
and claws its way up the inside of my pant legs,
finishing the job that her voice had begun an hour before
of dismantling my sense of ease and rightness in the evening.
The bar is half empty. This was long enough ago
that you could still smoke while sitting at your table,
and I light one as she slowly drains another shot of ouzo,
the achingly deliberate rolling of her wrist, then
the equally precise wiping of the back of the other wrist
across her mouth. In fact, this was long enough ago
that I had already "stopped drinking"—or rather,
that drinking had clubbed me into abstinence—
and I suddenly, vividly recall a night in the same bar,
a more distant time and woman sitting there
across from me, when in disgust I had watched myself
strain to complete a sentence with a full ten seconds
plodding by between each sodden word I spoke.
She beckons to the waitress, coral smeared
across her knuckles. *And now,* she says, *the mind*
fashions that you will drive me home,
and the mind does not fashion that you will sleep with me.
If this be youth with its glory passing into shade,
I think, give thanks, its dissolution overdue.
She reaches for my cigarette and knocks
the empty shot glass over.

Memento: For My Friend, a Carpenter, Whose Father Has Died

for Erhard Mahnke

When you are in your car
driving the darkening road
and the sadness strikes you,
when the lost face rises
from the shatterings of rain
that uncoil a pale longing
across your path,
when you are eating
your cold lunch
by the half-finished houses
and something leaves you
and you take up the handle
of the hammer and close
your grip on it slowly,
slowly—

when in a moment there
is the sea change, a draining
of blood-salt that harrows
your eyes to fire and water
and your cupped hands await
something that never comes—

remember, do not ever forget,
that the road you take is taking you
under the quavering stars,
that the rain is a thing
you wear in your hair
like dew crowning the trees in summer,
that the houses are patient,
the nail is straight,
the hands are in no need of waiting—

that your eyes are the father,
they are of the world
and are not,
and their seeing bears you
across the world and the water
to witness what all is not lost.

First Night, Perkins Pier

Here a woman draws a white coat close
against the cold. The sky
presents its chalice.
Pleas dissolve in smoke at the lips of
young children refusing to come in.

Nothing will change.
Each day plays the songs of
water, of bread, of dying.

Yet the winter lasts only a moment.
Edging the lake ice,
a girl tests her new skates,
ringing a silver bell, eating a coin of chocolate.

Ralph Culver

Signed Self-portrait: February

Knee-deep amid the clambering snows, the old
broom at parade rest in my grip, icebound,
I remark with odd admiration the gray rampart
the city plow blade grades across the mouth
of my driveway. From the porch roof by an empty
suet cage, a downy woodpecker goads me
with a glance. Well, he can wait a moment,
and so can my shovel, wherever it may be
under all this whiteness. With these bristles
seasons past have frayed and fretted to a bevel,
the broomstick vertical, I brush the only
Chinese ideogram I know—*increasing joy*—
into the surface of the snow beside the roses
patiently waiting in their burlap robes.

84

To March

Cutting carrots for soup, I'm distracted by the trees outside
      the window, their branches
making sweeping gestures through pale air half an hour before
      sundown,

officious yet somehow disinterested, the somber limbs
      directing, urging us to move
more quickly past the scene of some disaster or other and go
      about our business,

and I think, That's March, isn't it? They stand, the trees, above
      cracked plates of snow
that look like a pile of slate shingles just tumbled off a truck

and spilled around the trunks in shards. But that's March, too,
      the declining sunlight
suddenly flaring up across a glaze of ice that appears without
      warning

at a bend in the road, this unavoidable fact about yourself and
      the moment, and
you realize, as you turn the steering wheel smoothly into the
      skid, that

you are at ease with the prospect of any possibility. Everything
      in the bed
shifts as you hit dry pavement and then goes cascading, the
      whole load thunders overboard,

but you've stopped; stopped. Somehow, you're on all four
    tires. And when you climb
out of the cab, there is the wind, that storied, oft-venerated
    wind

moaning and clawing at your throat, a lover who wants you or
    wants you dead. Maybe both.
Probably both, I think, looking across the snow crust

gathering murk as dusk settles in, winter each day just a bit
    more distant, each day itself
just a bit longer and brighter than the last,

and return to the comfortable heft of the knife, the kitchen
    sweetened by steaming broth
and promise, another seeming catastrophe survived.

So Be It

Some kid's upside-down skateboard, the wheels still spinning.

Bordering the marsh, an empty field.
No. A redwing blackbird sways on the highest stalk.

I look at the back of my hand: flesh, the veins just beneath,
slanted sunlight over a stream in late autumn.

Hearing the blackbird's call before he calls.

And this hunger. How it goes on, and tomorrow, and always,
blazing up in the body, torching the years to ash.

Notes on the Poems

"First Night, Perkins Pier," page 83—An acrostic. The occasion for the poem is spelled in the first letter of each line, reading downward.

"For the Last Catamount," page 68—*Catamount* is another term for puma or mountain lion, in this instance the Eastern mountain lion of New England, finally declared extinct by the U.S. Department of the Interior in 2018. The catamount is an enduring part of the New England mythos, and sightings continue to be reported sporadically in the Green and White mountains.

Although the poem is not a tanka sequence in the usual sense, each stanza utilizes the tanka's 5-7-5-7-7 syllabic line structure, and each stanza is self-contained yet interrelated, another characteristic of the form in a sequence. Since ninth-century Japan, the tanka has been called upon to express love, longing, and regret, often in the context of the natural world, and that seemed to suit the poem's subject.

"Seamstress," page 62—An acrostic. The subject and dedicatee of the poem is spelled in the first letter of each line, reading downward.

Acknowledgments

Grateful acknowledgment is made to the editors of the print and online publications where many of these poems first appeared, several in slightly different form:

After Happy Hour Review, Albatross, The Alembic, Amoskeag, Bateau, Bear Creek Haiku, The Bitter Oleander, Common Ground Review, Denver Quarterly/Intro, 5 AM, The Kerf, Mud Season Review, North by Northeast, Off the Coast, Onion River Review, Plume, Route Seven, Seven Days, 10x3 Plus, Vermont Literary Review, Vermont Vanguard Press, The West Review, Willard & Maple, The Worcester Review

Thanks are also due to the following, which have reprinted several of these poems:

autumnskypoetrydaily.com, 3quarksdaily.com, *05401*

"For the Last Catamount" was selected for the anthology *So Little Time: Words and Images for a World in Climate Crisis,* ed. D. Cummings and G. Delanty, Green Writers Press, 2014.

"Memento: For My Friend, a Carpenter, Whose Father Has Died" and "Taking Bluegill at Lake Seneca" were selected for the anthology *Roads Taken: Contemporary Vermont Poetry,* third edition, ed. C. deNiord and S. Lea, Green Writers Press, 2021.

"Signed Self-portrait: February" was selected for reproduction as a limited-edition, hand-printed broadside by Chickadee Chaps & Broads (chickadeechaps.bigcartel.com) of Montpelier, Vermont, with illustrations by Gabriel Tempesta (gabrieltempesta.com).

Some of these poems appeared in two earlier chapbook collections: *Both Distances* (2013), which won the 2012 Anabiosis Press Chapbook Prize, and *So Be It* (WolfGang Press, 2018).

I am deeply grateful as a past grantee in poetry of the Vermont Arts Council (vermontartscouncil.org) for their consideration and financial support.

With special thanks to...

First, my parents. They have both passed on, and I miss them. No childhood is perfect, and mine had its share of heartache, anxiety, and trouble in which my father and mother played their part—my dad in particular. It took me many years, as it usually does, to realize how fortunate I was to have them as my parents, and I'm deeply grateful to them.

My sister, Carol. One thing about having a younger sibling is that it's often not until adulthood when you realize just how smart and insightful they are, and how much you have in common—truths I've now been privileged to know for a long time. I love you, and owe you so much for how you've hung in there with me through good and hard times. Thank you.

My extended family—especially my cousins Judy, Nina, Steve, and Pete—and my many friends. I'd have been lost a long time ago without you. Thank you.

My teachers, mentors, and guides. I may have been—often was—a less than exemplary student. I apologize for very possibly wasting your time and frustrating you in classroom and workshop settings. But every one of you became a trusted friend, and you each taught me your version of the most important lesson of all: that being a poet, in America, in our time, was a serious and vital calling. Just writing out your names makes me realize how absurdly fortunate I've been. At Goddard College in Vermont in the early 1970s: Paul Nelson, Marvin Bell, Barry Goldensohn, and Louise Glück. At the New School in New York City in the early 1970s: Daniel Halpern.

At the MFA Program for Writers at Warren Wilson College in North Carolina in the mid-1980s: Thomas Lux, Heather McHugh, and Ellen Bryant Voigt.

If we're lucky, and I am, we're blessed with champions of and believers in our work no matter how rough the going may get. I'm deeply grateful to you all, with a special nod to Beth Tucker, Jack and Margarita Pulaski, and Sydney Lea.

To the many individuals and organizations I've come to know, respect, and rely upon in the daily work of recognizing and correcting addictions and related compulsive behavior, thank you and keep the faith.

Marc Vincenz and MadHat Press. None of this is here now, in this form, in the reader's hands, if not for you. Ten-thousand thanks.

My children, Jason and Kate. You've brought an immeasurable, incalculable richness and meaning to my life. Anything worthwhile that I've done has been, in some way, for you. I am and will always be in your debt.

My beloved. You hill of wildflowers in my heart. *Tengo hambre de tu boca, de tu voz, de tu pelo....*

About the Author

RALPH CULVER was born in Illinois, raised in Pittsburgh, and for many years has lived in Vermont. He studied writing and literature at Goddard College (Plainfield, Vermont), the New School (New York City), and the MFA Program for Writers at Warren Wilson College (Swannanoa, North Carolina), and filmmaking at the University of Vermont. His poetry, fiction, and criticism have appeared in many publications and several anthologies, and he is a past grantee in poetry of the Vermont Arts Council among other awards and citations. His poetry collection *Both Distances* won the 2012 Anabiosis Press Chapbook Prize, and was followed in 2018 by the highly praised *So Be It* (WolfGang Press). *A Passable Man* is his first full-length collection.